Insects & Spiders

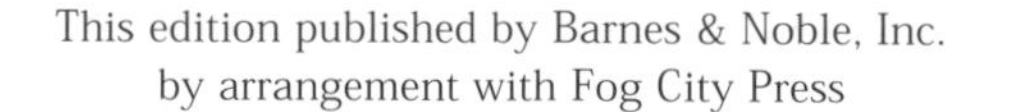

This edition published by Barnes & Noble, Inc.
by arrangement with Fog City Press

2003 Barnes & Noble Books
Copyright ©1997 Weldon Owen Pty Ltd

Published by Fog City Press
814 Montgomery Street
San Francisco, CA 94133 USA

Conceived and produced by Weldon Owen Pty Limited
59 Victoria Street, McMahons Point, NSW 2060, Australia
A member of the Weldon Owen Group of Companies
Sydney • San Francisco • Auckland • London

WELDON OWEN PUBLISHING
Publisher: Sheena Coupe
Creative Director: Sue Burk
Managing Editor: Rosemary McDonald
Project Editor: Kathy Gerrard
Designer: Karen Clarke

FOG CITY PRESS
Chief Executive Officer: John Owen
President: Terry Newell
Publisher: Lynn Humphries
Production Manager: Caroline Webber
Production Coordinator: James Blackman
Sales Manager: Emily Jahn
Vice President International Sales: Stuart Laurence

Text: Lesley Dow
Illustrators: Susanna Addario; Martin Camm; Simone End; Christer Eriksson; Giuliano Fornari; Jon Gittoes; Ray Grinaway; Tim Hayward/Bernard Thornton Artists, UK; Robert Hynes; David Kirshner; Frank Knight; James McKinnon; John Richards; Trevor Ruth; Claudia Saraceni; Kevin Stead; Thomas Trojer; Rod Westblade

All rights reserved. Unauthorized reproduction,
in any manner, is prohibited.
A catalog record for this book is available from
the Library of Congress, Washington. D.C.

First printed 2003

M 10 9 8 7 6 5 4 3

ISBN 0-7607-4641-9

Color reproduction by Colourscan Co Pte Ltd
Printed by SNP Leefung Printers limited (China)
Printed in China

A Weldon Owen Production

Insects & Spiders

CONSULTING EDITORS

George Else
& specialist Staff
Department of Entomology
The Natural History Museum
London

Contents

• INSECT INSPECTION •

• STAYING ALIVE •

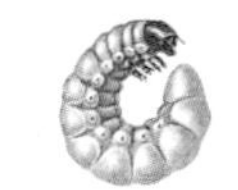

• CYCLES OF LIFE •

• AN INSECT'S WORLD •

• THE BIG ORDERS •

• INSECTS AND PEOPLE •

• SPOTLIGHT ON SPIDERS •

The Great Success Story

Insects are among the most successful creatures in the living world. They first appeared more than 400 million years ago, and fossilized specimens, such as the dragonfly at left, show that some have changed little over this time. More than a million species of insect have been identified, which means that they outnumber all other animal species put together. Even more await discovery, and some scientists think that the total number of species may be as high as 10 million. There are several reasons for these tremendous numbers, but the most important is size. Because insects are so small, individuals need only tiny amounts of food. They eat many different things, including wood, leaves, blood and other insects, and they live in a great range of habitats. The survival of insects is also helped by the ability of some to fly, and by their ability to endure tough conditions. Some desert insects can cope with temperatures above 104°F (40°C), and many insect eggs can survive temperatures much colder than a freezer.

TAKING OFF
Insects were the first animals that were able to fly. Cockchafers use their wings to escape danger. This male may also fly far in search of a mate.

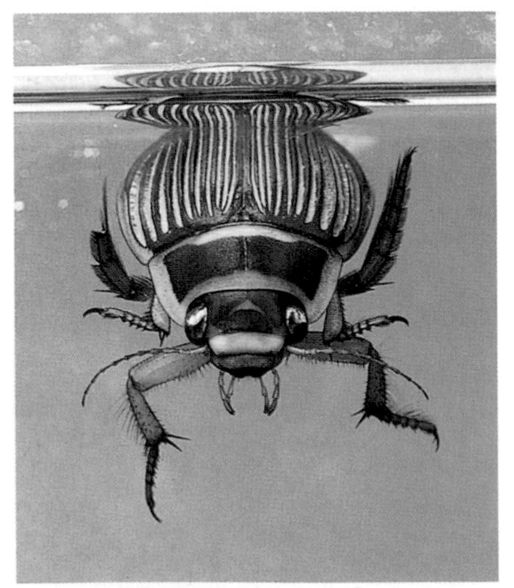

UNDERWATER INSECTS
Although insects are common in fresh water, hardly any are found in the sea. This diving beetle is one of many insects that live in fresh water.

LIVING TOGETHER
Many insects gather in groups for part of their lives. This swarm of hungry locusts may have more than a billion individuals, who can munch through huge quantities of food.

THE INSECT ARMY
Scientists divide insects into about 30 different groups, called orders. Insects from some of the most important orders are shown here.

Did You Know?

Many insects are so light that gravity has little effect on them. They run up vertical surfaces almost as easily as they run down them. If they do lose their grip and fall, they are rarely injured when they hit the ground.

Small Living Spaces

The way insects are built means that their bodies need to be small and light, or they would become too heavy to move. As shown on this graph, most insect species are less than 1 in (25 mm) long. However, even long insects can still be very light. The goliath beetle weighs no more than 3½ ounces (100 g). Insects have turned being small into an advantage by exploiting places that are too cramped for larger animals. These places include the space between the upper and lower surfaces of leaves, and the tiny gaps among particles of soil.

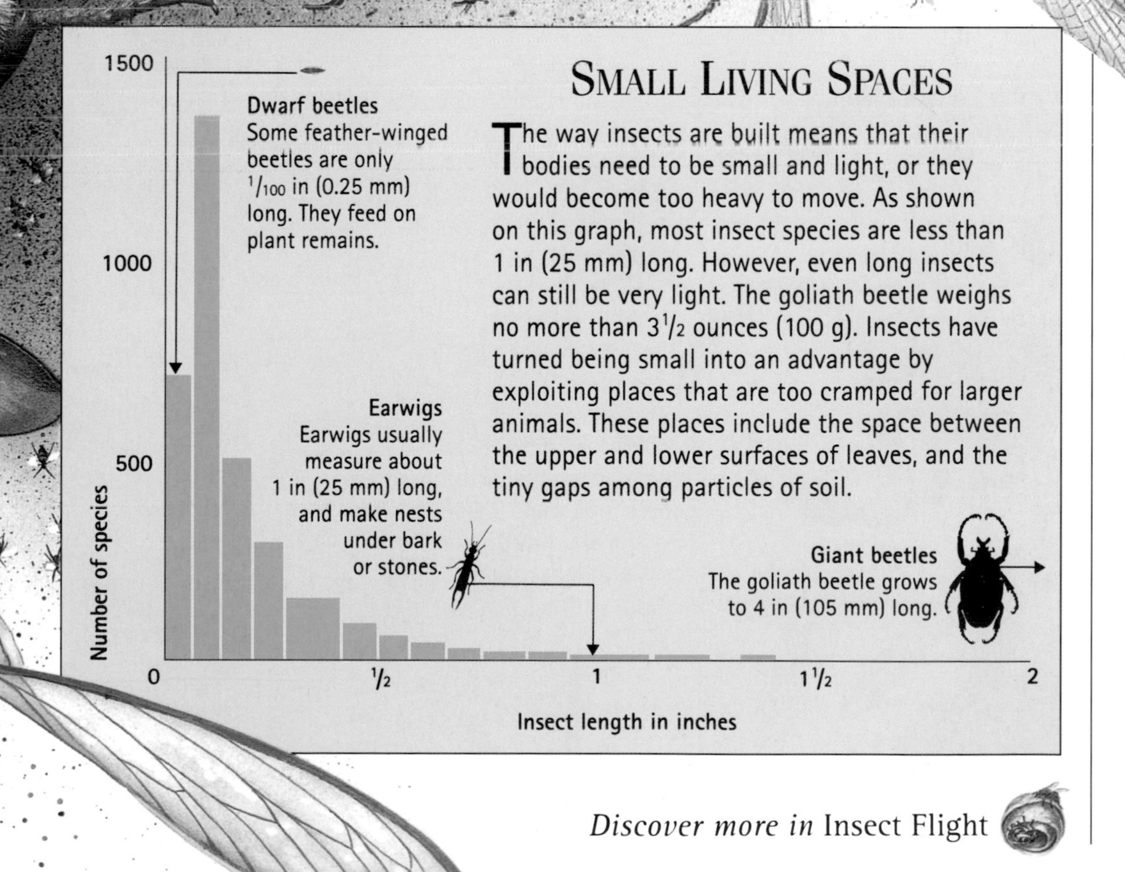

Discover more in Insect Flight

What is an Insect?

Insects belong to a group of animals called arthropods. All arthropods have a protective, hard body case, or exoskeleton. It covers the whole body, and is made up of separate plates that meet at flexible joints. An arthropod's muscles are attached to the inside of its exoskeleton, and they pull against the plates to make the body move. An insect's body is divided into three basic parts—head, thorax and abdomen. In adult insects, the head carries a pair of antennae, the eyes and a set of mouthparts. The thorax carries three pairs of legs and, usually, two pairs of wings. The abdomen contains the insect's digestive system, the organs used for reproduction and the sting organs—if the insect can sting. An insect's exoskeleton is made of a substance called chitin, which is like a natural plastic. It is usually covered with waxy substances that help prevent the insect from drying out.

Ocellus
Three simple eyes, or ocelli, detect the amount of light in the bee's surroundings.

Head
This consists of several interlocking plates and is one of the strongest parts of the body.

Mouthparts
Jaws, or mandibles, handle food and guide it into the insect's mouth.

Antenna
Antennae are delicate sensory organs that help the insect feel, smell, taste and hear.

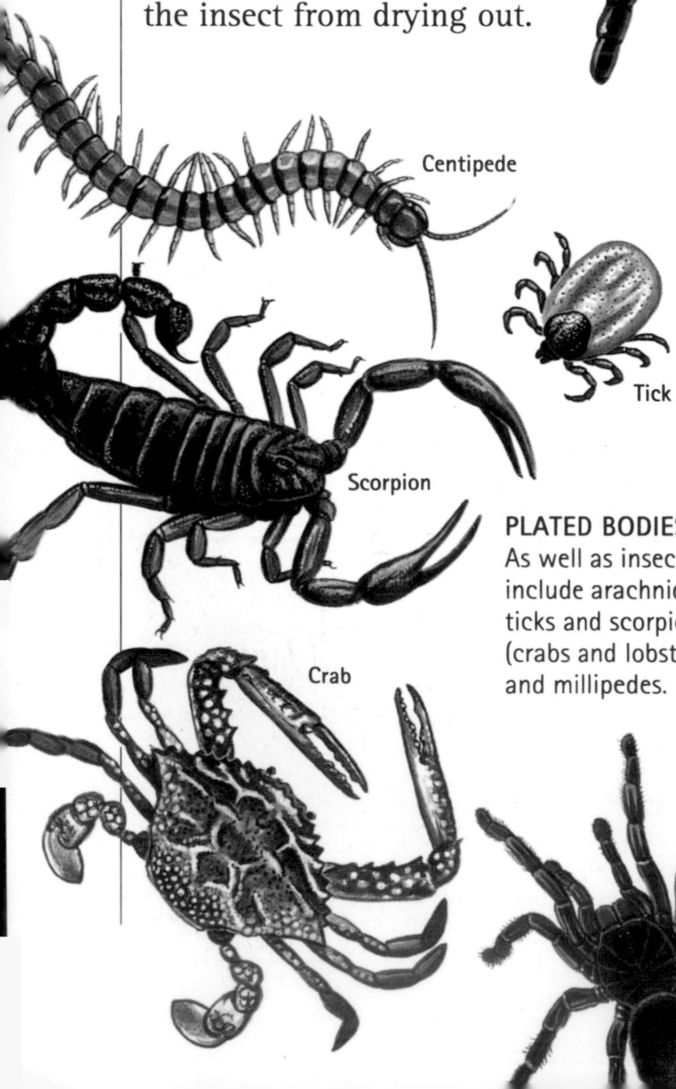

Eye
Adult insects have compound eyes made up of many small eyes packed together.

Thorax
This contains powerful muscles that operate the wings and legs.

Centipede

Tick

Scorpion

Crab

Spider

PLATED BODIES
As well as insects, arthropods include arachnids (spiders, mites, ticks and scorpions), crustaceans (crabs and lobsters), centipedes and millipedes.

Did You Know?

A flea can jump 100 times its own height. Before a jump, it uses its muscles to squeeze special rubber-like pads in its thorax. When it releases the pads, they spring back into shape and catapult the flea into the air.

REPEATING PATTERN
An insect's body is made up of plates arranged in segments. These segments are easy to see on the abdomen of this cockroach.

Wing
Insect wings are supported by thickened veins. The pattern of veins varies in different insects.

PRIMITIVE INSECT
A silverfish does not have wings or ocelli. Its flattened body allows it to wriggle into small crevices, even between the pages of a book.

Abdomen
More flexible than the head or thorax, this expands when the insect feeds.

Leg
In some insects, the three pairs of legs are very different in size. They are all attached to the thorax.

Foot
Hooks, pads and suckers on the feet allow insects to cling onto surfaces or to catch food.

A TYPICAL INSECT
A worker honeybee is a typical flying insect, with two pairs of wings and six legs. Its body is divided into three basic parts: the head, thorax and abdomen.

New Skins

Our skeleton grows in step with the rest of our body, but once an insect's exoskeleton has hardened, it cannot become any larger. In order to grow, the insect has to molt, or shed, its "skin," and replace it with a new one. During molting, the old exoskeleton splits open and the insect crawls out. The insect then takes in air or water, so that its body expands before the new exoskeleton becomes hard. Some insects molt more than 25 times, while others molt just twice. Once an insect becomes an adult, it usually stops molting and does not grow any more.

Q: Why do insects shed their exoskeletons?

Discover more in Getting Started

A Closer View

Inside an insect's body, many different systems are at work. Each one plays a part in keeping the animal alive and in allowing it to breed. One of the largest, the digestive system, provides the insect with fuel from its food. It is based around the gut, or alimentary canal, which runs the whole length of the body. When an insect eats, food is stored in a bulging part of the canal, called the crop. It then travels into the midgut, where it is broken down and absorbed. Leftover waste moves on to the anus and is expelled. The insect's circulatory system uses blood to carry digested food, but not oxygen, around the body. The blood is pumped forwards by a heart arranged along a muscular tube, but it flows back again through the body spaces among the body organs. The nervous system and the brain ensure that all the other systems work together. They collect signals from the sense organs, and carry messages from one part of the body to another.

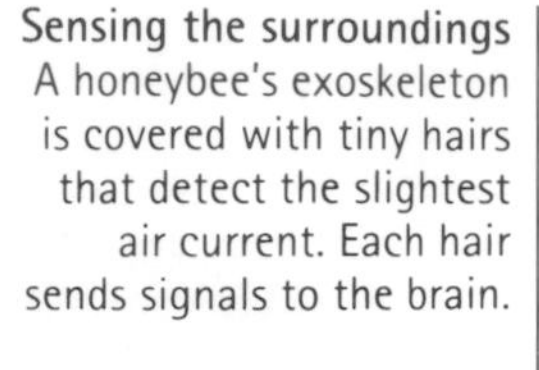

Sensing the surroundings
A honeybee's exoskeleton is covered with tiny hairs that detect the slightest air current. Each hair sends signals to the brain.

Trachea

Control center
An insect's brain collects signals from the eyes and other sense organs, and coordinates its body. It is connected to the nerve cord.

Power plant
The muscles in the thorax power the bee's wings and legs. Like all the bee's muscles, they are bathed in blood.

Mini-brain
Swellings, called ganglia, are arranged at intervals along the nerve cord. These control sections of the body.

Liquid meals
The bee uses its tongue like a drinking straw to suck up sugary nectar from flowers.

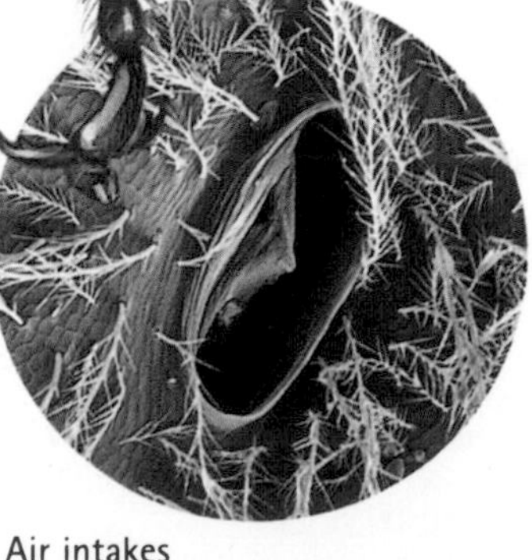

Air intakes
Openings, called spiracles, let air into the bee's internal air tubes (tracheae). Each spiracle has hairs to keep out dust and water.

INSIDE A BEE
This illustration shows major body systems of the worker honeybee. The digestive system is colored cream, the respiratory system white, the nervous system gray and the circulatory system green.

GETTING A GRIP
Each fly's foot has a pair of claws and bristly pads. The claws allow the fly to grip rough surfaces, while the bristly pads help it to cling onto smooth surfaces.

Hooked together
A honeybee has two pairs of wings. The larger front wings are joined to the smaller back wings by a row of hooks. The two pairs of wings beat together.

Strong wings
The wings are made of chitin, the same material as the rest of the exoskeleton. In some insects, the wings are covered in tiny hairs.

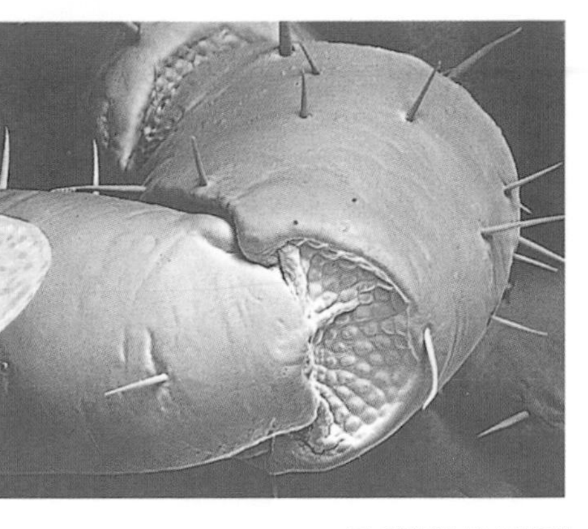

FLEXIBLE LEGS
Like all arthropods, an insect's leg has flexible joints that allow the leg to bend. This is the leg joint of a human head louse.

Midgut refueling
Food is digested and absorbed here. Insects that eat solid food have a muscular pouch (gizzard) where food is ground up before being digested.

Heart

Poison sac

Crop

Nerve cord

Shake a leg
This set of muscles in the bee's leg pulls on a long tendon to move the claws.

Sting

Fine Tracheae

Like all animals, insects need to breathe—take in oxygen and get rid of carbon dioxide. Because their blood does not carry oxygen, and they do not have lungs, insects breathe with the help of tiny air tubes called tracheae. The openings of these tubes, called spiracles, are located on the sides of the thorax and abdomen. Each trachea divides into many branches that eventually become so fine they go inside cells. When an insect molts, it sheds the linings of its tracheae through its spiracles. This caterpillar is undergoing this remarkable process.

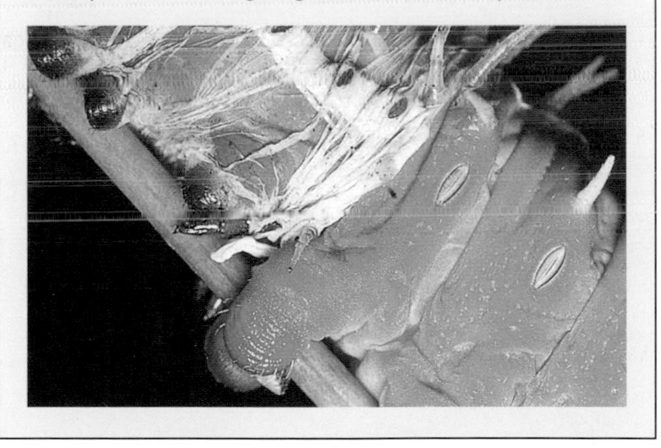

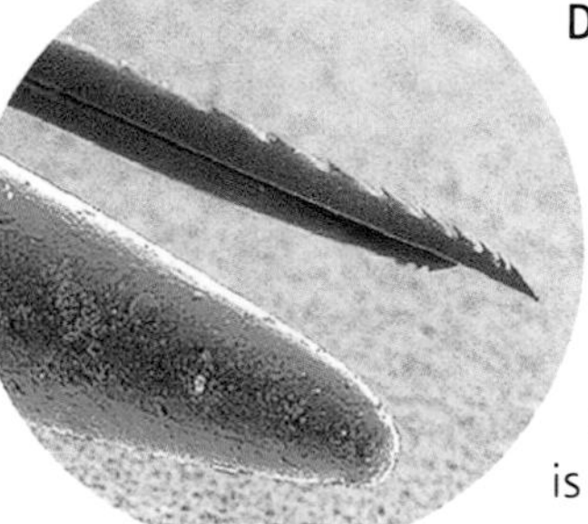

DEADLY WEAPON
A honeybee's sting is like a sharp rod with hooks on it. Once embedded in the skin, the sting releases its poison. Here, the sting (top) is compared to a needle.

Did You Know?

All insects are protected by body cases, but in larvae (grubs), the case is often quite thin. These lily beetle larvae shield themselves from their enemies with a protective coat made from their own droppings.

Discover more in Insect Senses

Q: How do insects get the oxygen they need?

SENSORY SKILLS

The shape of antennae varies among insects, and sometimes even between males and females of the same species.

Night-time feeder
A long-horned beetle's long antennae are used for feeling its way in the dark.

Seeking a mate
In flight, a male cockchafer's antennae open out to detect the scent of a female.

Damp skin spots
The human louse uses its antennae to sense damp parts of a body where it feeds on blood.

Air detector
Each butterfly antenna is a slender shaft ending with a small knob. The shafts are covered with hairs that detect air currents.

Hot spots
A female mosquito's feathery antennae sense heat from warm-blooded animals. This enables her to find food in the dark.

Feathery sniffer
A male emperor moth can smell a female more than 2 miles (3 km) away.

• STAYING ALIVE •

Insect Senses

To survive, an insect has to know about the world around it. It must be able to find food, track down a mate and, most important of all, detect its enemies before they have a chance to attack. Like many other animals, insects have five main senses—sight, hearing, smell, touch and taste. Each type of insect specializes in using some of these senses more than others. Because dragonflies and horseflies fly during the day, they have large eyes that help them find their victims. Most moths, on the other hand, fly at night. Instead of using sight, they find their food and partners by smell. As well as using senses to find out about the world, insects also have senses that monitor their own bodies. These tell them which way up they are flying, how their wings and legs are positioned, and whether they are speeding up or slowing down. For flying insects, these senses are particularly important.

Human's view

Bee's view

SEEING THE INVISIBLE

Many insects see wavelengths of light that are invisible to us. Above right is how a bee may view a flower. It gives more detail than a human view and guides the bee to the nectar.

Simple eyes
Known as ocelli, these small eyes on the top of the head sense the difference between sunlight and shade.

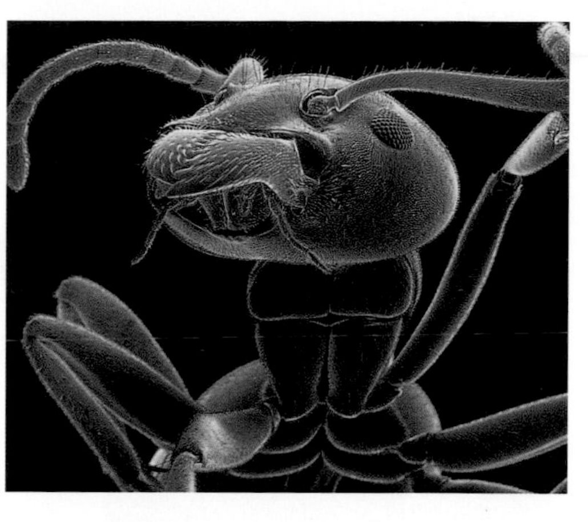

SMALL EYES
The more eyelets an insect has, the more clearly it sees. This wingless worker ant lives in the dark and has small compound eyes, which contain only a few hundred eyelets.

Feeling the heat
A horsefly's antennae are sensitive to heat, and are used to locate areas of exposed skin on a warm-blooded animal.

Making up a picture
The horsefly's compound eyes each contain several thousand eyelets. The fly's brain combines the signals from the eyelets to make up an image of the surroundings.

Ears on the Body

Insects often use their antennae to hear, but they also have other ways of detecting different sounds and vibrations.

Ears on legs
Bush crickets have ears on their front legs. Each ear is a thin oval membrane that moves when the air vibrates.

Feeling the ground
Ants sense vibrations through their legs. They often respond to these vibrations by preparing to attack an enemy.

Ears on the abdomen
Grasshoppers and locusts have ears on their abdomen. They are particularly sensitive to the calls made by their own species.

Leg bristles
A cockroach uses special bristles to sense the vibrations made by something moving towards it.

Wings as ears
The thin and delicate wings of a lacewing pick up vibrations in the air and sense movements.

LOOKING FOR BLOOD
Female horseflies feed on blood, and they rely mainly on vision to track down a meal. Like most insects, they have compound eyes, which are made of many smaller eyes, called eyelets, packed tightly together.

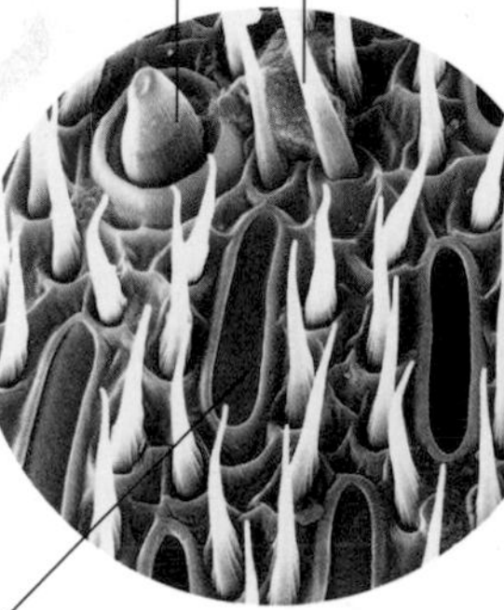

MULTIPURPOSE ANTENNAE
This magnified picture shows the surface of a wasp's antenna. These antennae carry taste buds for sensing food, sensors that smell the air, and hairs that respond to touch.

Discover more in Insect Flight 

Food and Feeding

Individually, insects are quite choosy about what they eat, but together they devour a vast range of different foods. Many insects feed on plants or on small animals, but some survive on more unusual food, including rotting wood, blood, horns or even wool. To tackle each of these foods, insects have a complicated set of specially shaped mouthparts. A praying mantis, for example, has sharp jaws, or mandibles, that stab and cut up its captives, while its other mouthparts help to hold the food and pass it towards the mouth. A grasshopper has similar mouthparts, but its main jaws are much stronger and blunter, and so are ideal for crushing the plant material it prefers. The mouthparts of insects that feed on liquids often look very different than those of insects that live on solid foods. A mosquito has a long stylet that works like a syringe, while a butterfly or moth has a long tongue, or proboscis, which acts like a drinking straw. As this butterfly (above left) demonstrates, the tongue conveniently coils up when not in use.

LIVING DRILL
The hazelnut weevil has a long, slender "snout" with tiny jaws at the tip. Using its jaws like a drill, the weevil chews holes in hazelnuts.

MIDAIR REFUELING
With its tongue uncoiled, a hawk moth drinks nectar from deep inside a flower. Some hawk moths have tongues that are more than 6 in (15 cm) long.

CHANGING TASTES
Larvae and adult insects often eat very different foods. An adult potter wasp feeds on nectar whereas its larva (left top) feeds on caterpillars.

Insect Mouthparts

Insect mouthparts are like tools in a toolkit. They are specially shaped to gather particular food and allow it to be swallowed.

Spongy pads
Houseflies use a spongy pad to pour saliva over their food. After the food has dissolved, it is sucked up.

Piercing mouthparts
Female mosquitoes use their needle-like mouthparts to stab through the skin and suck up blood. Males sip only plant juices.

Powerful jaws
Many ants have strong jaws for gripping and cutting up small animals. Some can slice through human skin.

FAST FOOD
A locust chops through a tasty leaf quickly. Its mouthparts, called palps, explore the leaf as it eats.

Did You Know?

This darkling beetle lives in Africa's Namib Desert, where the only moisture comes from mist rolling in from the sea. To get water, the beetle points its abdomen into the wind, and collects the moisture that condenses on its body.

MOPPING UP
Before it can eat, a housefly must pour saliva over its food. The saliva often dries to form small spots that can be seen after the fly has moved on.

PATIENT KILLER
A praying mantis surprises its victims by striking out with its front legs. The legs snap shut and help grip the prey with sharp spines. The mantis often begins to feed even while its catch is still struggling to escape.

Q: Why do insects have different kinds of mouthparts?

FEROCIOUS TWIG
Most caterpillars eat plants for food, but this looper moth caterpillar catches other insects. Camouflaged to look like a twig, it attacks small flies when they land nearby.

DEADLY DASH
After cockroaches, tiger beetles are among the fastest sprinters of the insect world. Moving at more than 1½ ft (0.5 m) per second, this tiger beetle is chasing some ants. The beetle's large jaws will quickly snatch and crush the ants.

Predators and Parasites

One third of all insects feed on other animals, either as predators or parasites. Predators catch their prey by hunting it actively, or lying in wait until food comes within reach. Some of the most spectacular hunters feed in the air. Dragonflies, for example, swoop down and snatch up other flying insects with their long legs. On the ground, active hunters include fast-moving beetles, as well as many ants and wasps. Some wasps specialize in hunting spiders, which they sting—sometimes after a fierce battle. Insects that hunt by stealth, or lying in wait, are usually harder to spot. These include mantises and bugs, which are often superbly camouflaged to match their background. A few of these stationary hunters build special traps to catch their food. Antlion larvae dig steep-sided pits in loose soil and wait for ants to tumble in. Insects that are parasites live on or inside another animal, called the host, and feed on its body or blood. The host animal can sometimes be harmed or killed.

EASY PICKINGS
Hunting is sometimes easy work. Because aphids move very slowly, they cannot escape hungry ladybugs.

UNDERWATER ATTACK
Only a few insects are large enough to kill vertebrates (animals with backbones). This diving beetle has managed to catch a salamander.

DEATH OF A BEE
Assassin bugs use their sharp beak to stab their victims and then suck out the body fluids. This one has caught a honeybee by lying in wait inside a flower.

CLEANING UP

Instead of hunting live animals, burying beetles feed on dead bodies. They bury carcasses, then feed themselves and their larvae on the remains.

DINING IN

Parasitic insects use living animals as fresh food. Many lay their eggs on the larvae of other insects, or inject eggs through the skin of the victim. When the eggs hatch, these larvae feed on their host. They start with the less essential parts of the host's body, so that it survives for as long as possible. Eventually, they burst out through the host's skin and turn into adults. This hawk moth caterpillar has been feasted on by parasitic wasps, and is covered with their empty cocoons.

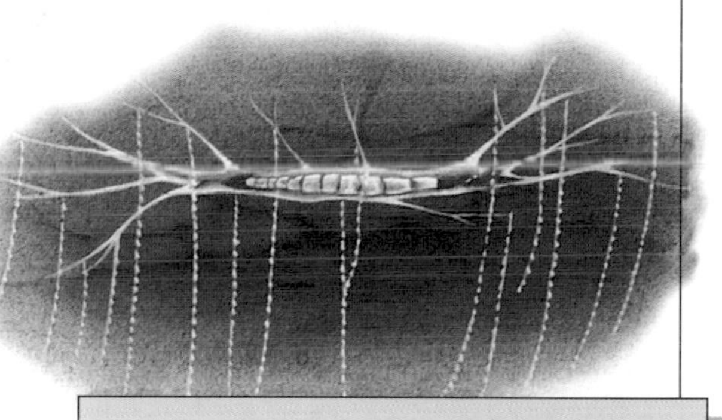

DID YOU KNOW?

The larvae of fungus gnats, found in caves in New Zealand, catch flying insects by glowing in the dark. Each larva produces a thread of sticky mucus that traps insects as they fly towards the glowing light. The larva then eats the insect and the trap.

Q: How do insects that lie in wait catch their food?

Insects and Plants

When insects first appeared on Earth, they found a world brimming with plants. Over millions of years, insects and plants evolved side by side. During this time, some insects became deadly enemies of plants, but others became valuable partners in the struggle for survival. Insects use plants for many things, but the most important of all is for food. Different insects eat all parts of plants, from roots and stems to leaves and flowers. Most of them eat living plants, but some help to break down plants once they are dead. By doing this, insects help to recycle important nutrients so that other plants can use them. Insects also live on or in plants, and they often damage plants when they set up home. Despite this insect attack, plants are not completely defenseless. Many use sticky hairs or chemicals to keep insects away, and some even catch insects and digest them. However, not all visitors are unwelcome. When bees feed at flowers, they carry pollen from plant to plant. This helps plants to pollinate and spread to new areas.

FLYING COURIER
Bees, butterflies, moths and wasps are all common visitors to flowers. These insects become dusted with pollen while they feed on the sugary nectar of the flowers.

GETTING A GRIP
Caterpillars have to hang on tight while they feed. They do this with special "legs" that end in sucker-like pads. They lose these legs when they become moths or butterflies.

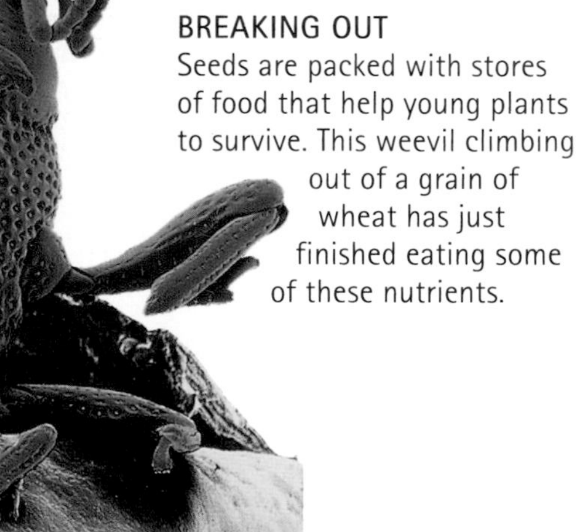

BREAKING OUT
Seeds are packed with stores of food that help young plants to survive. This weevil climbing out of a grain of wheat has just finished eating some of these nutrients.

SLOW GROWTH
The larva of a stag beetle spends its entire early life hidden inside rotting wood. Because wood is not very nutritious, it takes the larva a long time to mature.

Strange but True

The caterpillars of one Mexican moth grow inside the beans of a small bush. If a bean falls onto warm, sunny ground, the caterpillar inside jerks its body to make the bean "jump" into the shade. Each bean can move up to 2 in (5 cm) in a single hop.

LEAFY FEAST

Eating side by side, beetle larvae chew away at a leaf. Insects kill some plants, but enough plants are always left to allow both plants and insects to survive.

BUILDING WITH LEAVES

Female leafcutter bees clip out pieces of leaf with their jaws, and take the pieces back to their nests. They use them to make tube-shaped cells for larvae.

Plants That Eat Insects

In order to grow, plants need substances called mineral nutrients. They usually get these from the ground, but some plants that live where nutrients are scarce also get them from the bodies of insects. This sundew has trapped a fly in its sticky hairs, and will soon digest its prey. Other carnivorous plants catch insects in fluid-filled traps, or with leaves that suddenly snap shut.

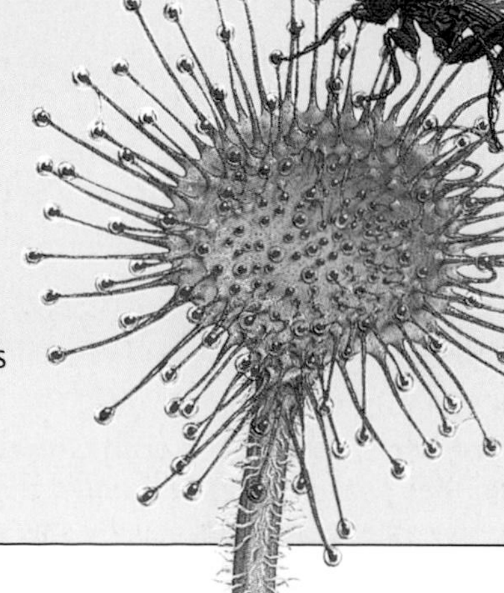

Insect Defense

For insects, the world is full of danger. They are under constant threat of being eaten, and their enemies include not only birds, lizards and spiders, but also other insects. Many insects defend themselves by hurrying away at the first sign of trouble. Others stay still and well hidden. They hide in soil or rotting wood, or make themselves look like the objects around them. Some insects imitate thorns, sticks, leaves and even animal droppings, and they are often invisible until they move. Another line of defense works in a completely different way. Instead of hiding, some insects are brightly colored and easy to see, like the caterpillar on the left. But their colors warn predators that they are unpleasant or even dangerous to eat. Insects like this, however, are not always what they seem. Some harmless insects imitate those that have a bad taste, and others look just like those with a dangerous sting. If all these defenses fail, some insects stand their ground and attack. With their armored bodies, sharp jaws and toxic chemicals, they often live to fight another day.

BATTLE POSTURE
This wood ant prepares for battle by thrusting its abdomen upwards. When an attacker comes closer, the ant squirts it with a stream of acid from the tip of its abdomen.

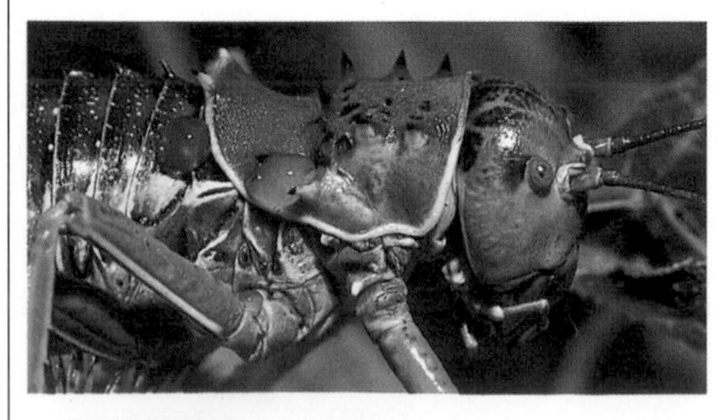

SICKLY SCENT
When some insects, such as this bush cricket, are threatened, they ooze droplets of a liquid that has a repulsive smell. Attackers usually stay away.

Mottled beauty
With wings spread out, the moth blends into the tree bark.

Bark bug
This has a flat, patterned body like the surface of tree bark.

Leaf insect
The flattened body and forewings mimic a single leaf.

Stick insect
Slow movements help a stick insect to look like part of a plant.

Sword-grass butterfly caterpillar
The caterpillar's slender green body is well hidden among blades of grass.

Comma butterfly
Ragged brown wings imitate the color and shape of dead leaves.

Long-headed grasshopper
The grasshopper's pointed head gives it a sticklike outline.

BLENDING IN
Insects are experts in the art of camouflage. This scene shows how 13 different insects use camouflage to avoid being spotted.

STARING EYES
Many moths have two large spots on their back wings. When disturbed, they reveal the spots, which look like two eyes set in a menacing face.

Strange but True

It is hard to imagine an insect imitating a snake, but this is how some swallowtail caterpillars defend themselves. On their back, they have two large eyespots, which make them look like a small poisonous snake.

Defense Plans

There is no such thing as one completely successful defense plan. Many insects have several ways to defend themselves. If one method is not successful, they will try another. The puss moth caterpillar relies initially on camouflage, but if an attacker sees it, the caterpillar moves onto the next plan. This involves inflating its head, and producing a pair of "horns" to frighten its attacker. If the caterpillar is still in danger, it squirts a spray of acid at its attacker, from a gland just beneath the head.

Emerald moth caterpillar
The body projections make this caterpillar look like a twig with buds.

Swallowtail butterfly larva
The texture and shape of the larva's body look like bird droppings.

Bush cricket
The veined front wings are pressed together to look like an upright leaf.

Flower mantis
This mantis is the same color as the flower. It is disguised as it waits to catch prey.

Angle shades moth
The wings look like a newly fallen leaf.

Cryptic grasshopper
The round outline and mottled colors imitate a small pebble.

KICKING BACK
The giant weta from New Zealand raises its powerful back legs to show that it can fight back. These legs have large spines.

Getting Started

Animals begin life in two different ways. Some develop inside their mother's body until they are ready to be born. Others, including most insects, develop from eggs outside their mother's body. Before a female insect can lay her eggs, she normally has to mate. Once this has happened, she chooses a place for her eggs, making sure that each one is near a source of suitable food. In most cases, she then abandons them, and makes no attempt to look after her young. However, not all insects start life this way. A few female insects can reproduce without needing to mate. Some insects give birth to live young, such as aphids who give birth to nymphs, and tsetse flies who give birth to larvae. A few insects are careful parents and take care of their eggs. Female earwigs lay small clutches of eggs and look after them by licking them clean. Many bugs carry their eggs on their backs, and guard their young after they hatch.

DANGEROUS MOMENT
Male insects are often smaller than females, and some have to be careful when they mate. Unless he is careful, this male mantis will end up as a meal for his partner.

FOOD FOR THE YOUNG
Insects often use their sense of smell to find good places for their eggs. This dead mouse has attracted blowflies that are ready to lay eggs.

A QUEEN'S LIFE
In an ant colony, only one individual—the queen—lays eggs. The eggs are carried away by worker ants, who tend and feed the young after they hatch. Most termites also reproduce this way.

Did You Know?

Insects that give birth to live young have fast-growing families. Within a few days, a female leaf beetle or aphid can be surrounded by dozens of offspring. Unlike insects that start life as eggs, each one can feed right away.

EGGS ON THE MOVE
A female giant water bug glues her eggs onto the back of a male. While carrying the eggs, the male is unable to use his wings.

Insect Eggs

Insect eggs are remarkable objects. Because they are so small, it is often difficult to see them without a microscope. A few insects drop their eggs from the air, but most glue them firmly to something that will provide food for their young. Insect eggs are sometimes laid singly, but many are laid in clusters, with hundreds or even thousands of eggs side by side. A few insects make special structures to help their eggs survive. Cockroaches lay batches of eggs in special cases; green lacewings lay their eggs on slender stalks, which makes the eggs difficult for predators to reach. Some eggs hatch soon after they are laid, but others stay inactive during months of cold or dry weather, when all the adults may die.

Horsefly eggs

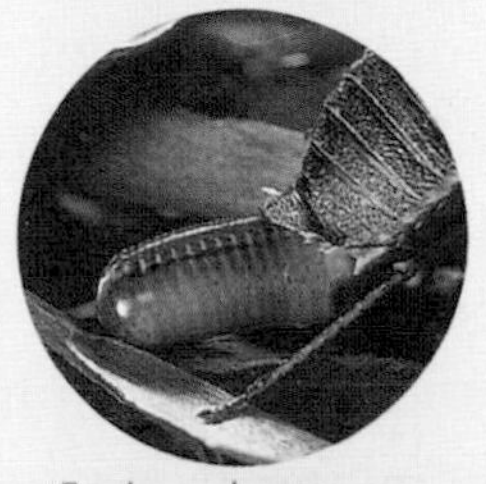

Eucalyptus tip bug eggs

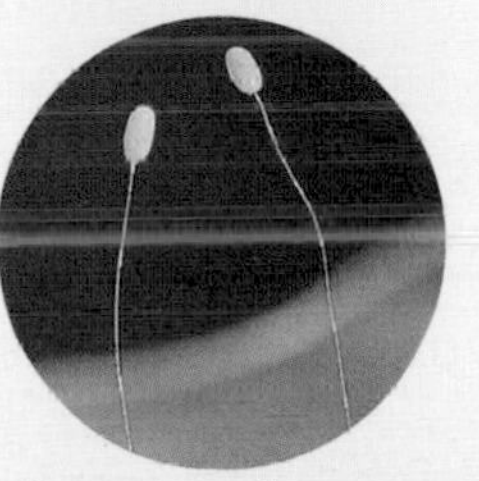

Cockroach egg case

Green lacewing eggs

A GOOD START
This female ichneumon wasp drills into a tree branch. She stings the larva of a wood wasp and deposits an egg through the tube, or ovipositor, onto the larva. When this egg hatches, it will feed on its unlucky host.

From Nymph to Adult

After an insect has hatched out of its egg, it starts to feed and grow. However, as well as growing, it often changes shape. This is called metamorphosis. In some insects, the changes are only slight, so the young insect looks much like the adult form. In others, the changes are so great that the young and adult look completely different. Insects that change only slightly include dragonflies, grasshoppers, earwigs, cockroaches, true bugs and praying mantises. Their young are called nymphs. A nymph does not have wings, although it does have small wing buds, and it is usually a different color from its parents. It often lives in a different habitat and feeds on different food. Most nymphs will molt several times. Each time a nymph sheds its skin, its body gets bigger and its wing buds become longer. Eventually, the nymph is ready for its final molt. It breaks out of its old skin, and emerges as an adult insect with working wings. It can then fly away to find a mate.

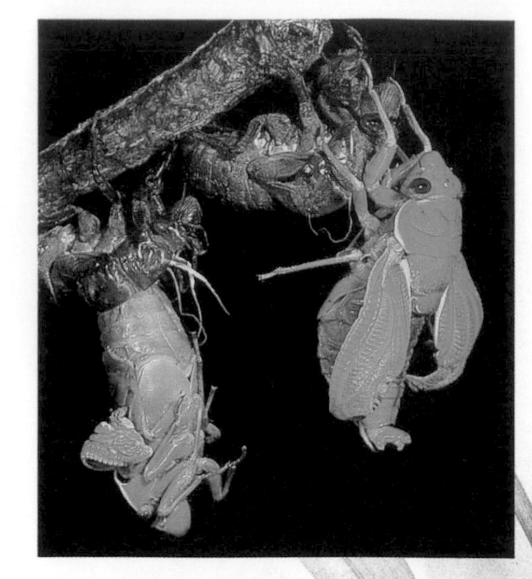

FINAL MOLT
After many years feeding underground as nymphs, these cicadas are shedding their skins for the last time. Their crumpled wings will soon expand and dry.

MANTIS MARCH
These newly hatched praying mantis nymphs look like miniature versions of their parents. They have well-developed legs, but their wing buds are still very small.

UNDERWATER NYMPHS
Adult dragonflies live in the air, but their nymphs develop under the water. Each nymph lives in water for up to five years before it hauls itself up a plant stem, sheds its skin for the last time, and emerges as an adult, able to fly.

Laying eggs
This dragonfly inserts her eggs into a water plant. Some species let the eggs fall to the bottom of ponds.

On the move
Dragonfly eggs can take several weeks to hatch. Each tiny nymph chews its way out of its egg case.

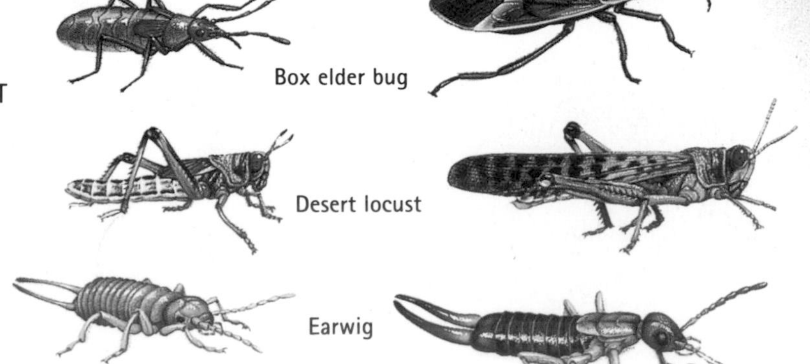

NYMPH TO ADULT
Like their parents (far right), nymphs have six legs. Their bodies change in proportion as they grow, but they keep the same overall shape.

BRIEF LIFE
This female mayfly has spent up to three years as a nymph, but will live for just one day as an adult. She cannot eat or drink, and her only purpose is to mate and lay eggs.

BREATHING UNDERWATER

Many insects spend a large part of their lives underwater. They all have to breathe, but they do so in different ways. Water scorpions and mosquito larvae get oxygen from the air, breathing through tubes that pierce the surface. Diving beetles and back swimmers collect bubbles of air at the surface, and carry them underwater when they swim. Dragonfly and damselfly nymphs use special flaps called gills to get their oxygen from the water. In dragonflies, the gills are inside the nymph's abdomen, but in damselflies, they stick out like small tails.

On patrol
An adult dragonfly has large eyes and is a powerful flier. It swoops over the water and catches other insects.

Drying time
The newly emerged adult rests in the sunshine while its wings expand and dry out.

Mating
A male (top left) and female come together to mate. Gripping the female just behind her head, the male fertilizes her eggs.

Leaving the water
Just before its final molt, the nymph climbs up a plant stem and out of the water.

Breaking out
The nymph swallows air to burst its old skin, and then eases itself out.

Hunter's diet
Using its special hinged jaws, the nymph catches tadpoles, worms and even small fish.

STRANGE BUT TRUE

In the United States there are two species of cicada that take either 13 or 17 years to mature underground. In response to some mysterious signal, millions of adults emerge together. They mate and lay eggs, and the cycle is repeated again.

A CHANGE OF LIFE
The atlas moth has four stages in its life cycle—egg, larva, pupa and adult. Larvae put all their energy into feeding, while adults mate and lay eggs.

Mating
A female's scent attracts a male, and the moths mate.

Laying eggs
The female moth searches for suitable food plants and glues her eggs to the leaves.

The next stage
A larva, or caterpillar, hatches from an egg. It grows bigger with several molts.

• CYCLES OF LIFE •

A Complete Change

Many young insects look quite unlike their parents. They do not have wings, and some do not even have legs. They often spend all their time on, or in, the things they eat. Young insects such as these are called larvae, and they include maggots, grubs and caterpillars. Compared to adult insects, they have soft bodies. Larvae protect themselves by tasting horrible, by being difficult to swallow, or by hiding away. A typical larva feeds for several weeks, shedding its skin several times while growing. When mature, its appetite suddenly vanishes, it stops moving and it becomes a pupa. The pupa has a tough outer case, and is sometimes protected by a silk cocoon. Inside the case, the larva's body changes dramatically. It is broken down and reassembled, so that it gradually turns into an adult insect. When this change, or metamorphosis, is complete, the case splits open and the adult insect, with wings, breaks out. It is now ready to reproduce.

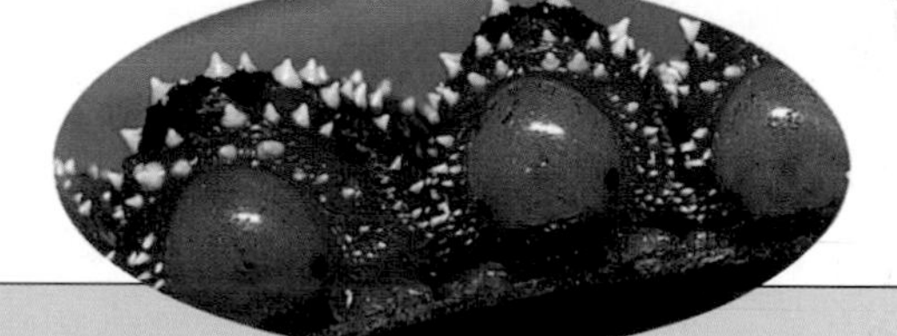

Did You Know?

Most larvae feed for many hours every day, and they put on weight very quickly. Just before they turn into pupae, fully grown larvae are often heavier than the adult insects of the same species.

LEGLESS LARVAE
Mosquito larvae live in water and feed on microscopic animals. They swim by wriggling their bodies, and breathe through short tubes.

Airborne
When its wing veins have hardened, the moth flies off.

Pupating
The caterpillar fastens itself in position with threads of silk.

Opening up
After breaking open the pupal case, the adult moth pumps blood into its wings.

Q: Whhat are the four stages of metamorphosis?

NATURAL SILK
Each silk moth cocoon is made of a single silk thread more than 1/2 mile (1 km) long. As soon as a moth emerges from its cocoon, it mates

PAMPERED UPBRINGING
Honeybee larvae mature inside wax cells, and worker bees bring food to them. These bees are turning into pupae, and will soon emerge as adults.

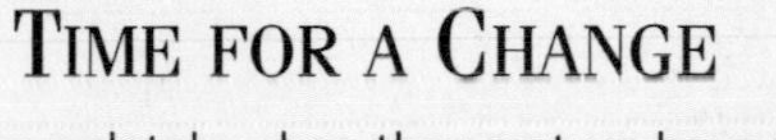

TIME FOR A CHANGE

Insects that change completely when they mature have four stages in their life cycles. Each stage usually lasts for a different length of time and these times vary from species to species. The stag beetle is a relatively slow developer, and spends many months as a larva hidden in wood, feeding only on rotting vegetation. The ladybug develops more quickly, and spends over half its life as an adult. The northern caddis fly spends most of its life as a larva. It lives in ponds and quiet waters in a specially constructed case.

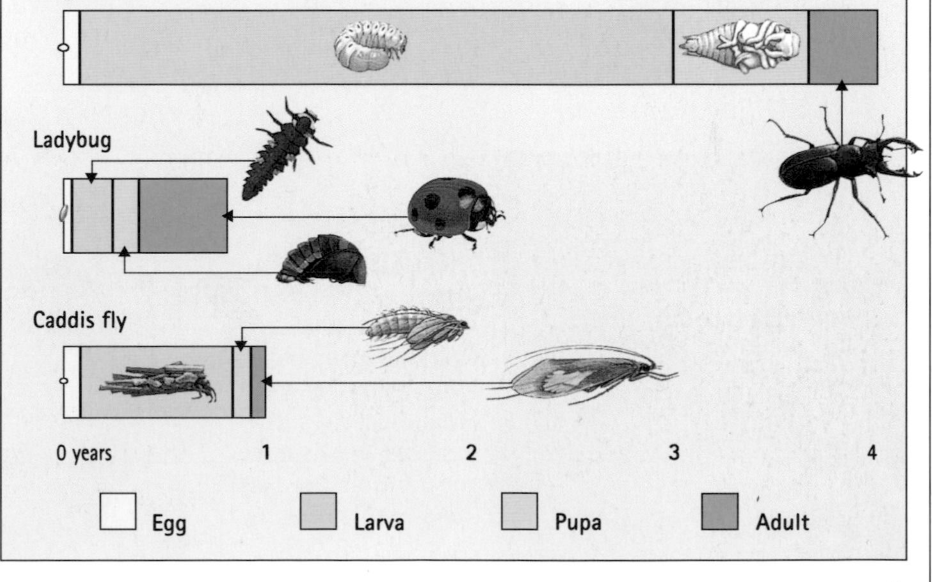

Discover more in The Great Success Story

Insect Flight

Insects were the first animals to fly. Today they share the air with birds and bats, but they are still the most numerous fliers in the animal world. Some insects fly on their own. Others, such as midges and locusts, gather in swarms. A swarm can contain just a few dozen insects, or more than a billion. Flying allows insects to escape from danger, and makes it easier for them to find mates. It is also a perfect way to reach food. Bees and butterflies fly among flowers, and hawk moths often hover in front of them. Dragonflies use flight to attack other insects in the air. They are the fastest fliers in the insect world, and can reach speeds of more than 31 miles (50 km) per hour. Most insects have two pairs of wings, made of the same material that covers the rest of their bodies. The wings are powered by muscles in the thorax. These muscles either flap the wings directly, or make the thorax move and this causes the wings to flap.

WINGS COMPARED
In most insects, the front and back wings look different. Insect wings are supported by branching veins, and are sometimes covered with tiny hairs or scales.

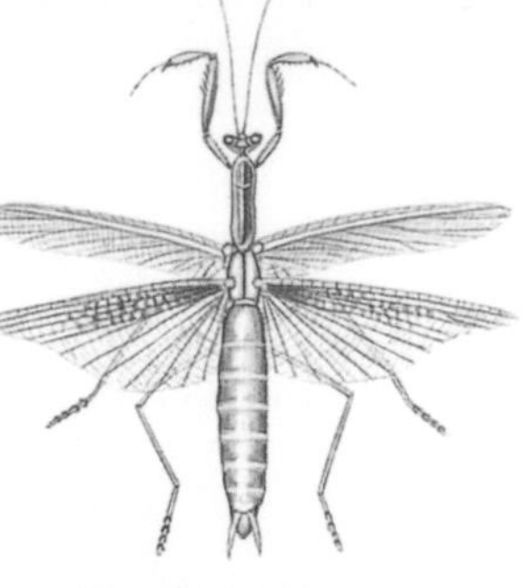

Pleated back wings
The back wings of a mantis fold up like fans when not in use.

Did You Know?

Insects such as thrips and aphids are too small and slow to make much headway on their own. Instead, they are carried by the wind, blowing them from one place to another far away.

VERTICAL TAKEOFF
Butterflies rest with their wings together. At takeoff, the wings peel apart, and the air sucks the butterfly upwards and away from danger.

REFUELING STOP
Flight is a fast and efficient way of getting about, but it uses a lot of energy. Many insects, such as bees, drink sugary nectar from flowers to give them energy.

Long-distance Travelers

Although insects are small animals, some of them travel huge distances in search of food or warmth. Dragonflies, locusts and moths often migrate, but the star travelers of the insect world are butterflies. In spring, North American monarch butterflies (left) set off northwards from Mexico. Many travel more than 1,500 miles (2,400 km). Painted lady butterflies set out from North Africa, and often make even longer journeys. Some of them manage to cross the Arctic Circle in Scandinavia, making a total distance of more than 1,800 miles (2,900 km).

Single pair of wings
Instead of back wings, true flies have tiny knobs called halteres.

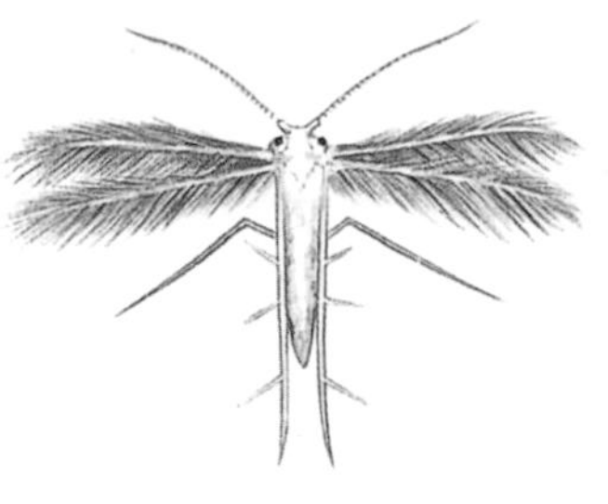

Plumed wings
Thrips and plume moths have wings that look like tiny feathers.

Hooked wings
A wasp's back and front wings are connected to each other by tiny hooks.

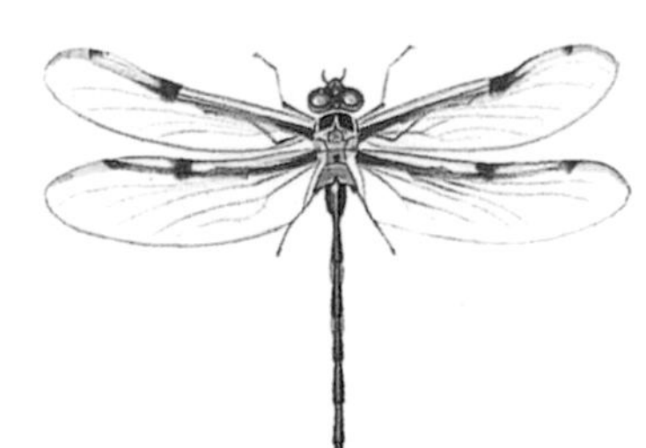

Double pair of wings
A dragonfly's front and back wings beat in opposite directions.

ASSISTED TAKEOFF

Weak fliers, such as this scorpion fly, often jump into the air from a high point. This assists them in gaining lift during takeoff.

FLY AWAY LADYBUG

Like all beetles, a ladybug has hardened front wings that do not beat up and down. They provide lift that helps the ladybug stay in the air.

Grounded
A ladybug's back wings are normally packed away under its hard front wings.

Making ready
Before it can fly, a ladybug opens its front wings and unfolds its back wings.

Takeoff!
The front wings swing outwards, and when the back wings are beating fast enough, the ladybug takes off.

LOOPING WALK
Some caterpillars move by holding the ground tight with their front legs, and pulling their body into a loop. They stretch forwards to straighten the loop, and then start the process again.

Did You Know?

Human head lice have such a strong grip that they are almost impossible to dislodge. They hang on tight even when hair is being washed or combed. Each leg ends in a claw that locks around a hair. Lice walk from head to head, laying eggs wherever they go.

Moving Around

Many people find insects alarming because of their sudden movements. Insects are not always fast, but because they weigh so little, most of them can stop and start far more suddenly than we can. The way an insect moves depends on where it lives. On land, the slowest movers are legless larvae. They have to wriggle to get around. Adult insects normally move using their legs, and they either walk or run, or jump into the air. The champion jumpers of the insect world are grasshoppers and crickets, but jumping insects also include fleas, froghoppers and some beetles. Tiny, wingless insects called springtails also jump, but instead of using their legs, they launch themselves by flicking a special "tail." Legs are useful in water, and insects have evolved a variety of leg shapes to suit watery ways of life. Water boatmen and diving beetles have legs like oars, and row their way through the water. Pond-skaters live on top of the water, and have long and slender legs that spread their weight over the surface.

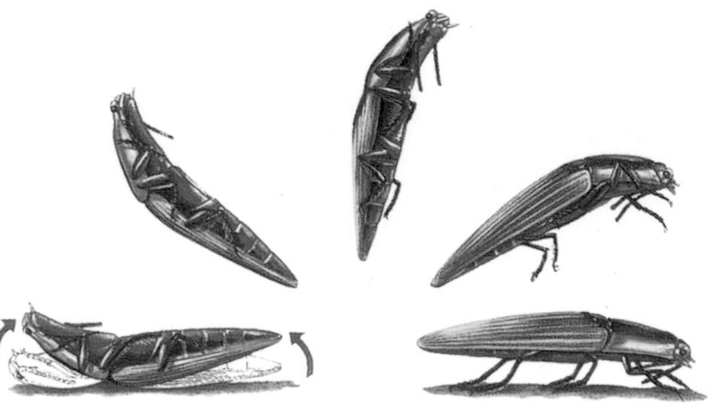

HEAD-BANGER
A click beetle escapes danger by lying on its back and keeping perfectly still (above left). If attacked its head suddenly snaps upwards, hurling it out of harm's way and back onto its feet.

WALKING IN THREES
Insects walk by moving three legs at a time—one on one side, and two on the other. This makes their bodies zigzag as they move along.

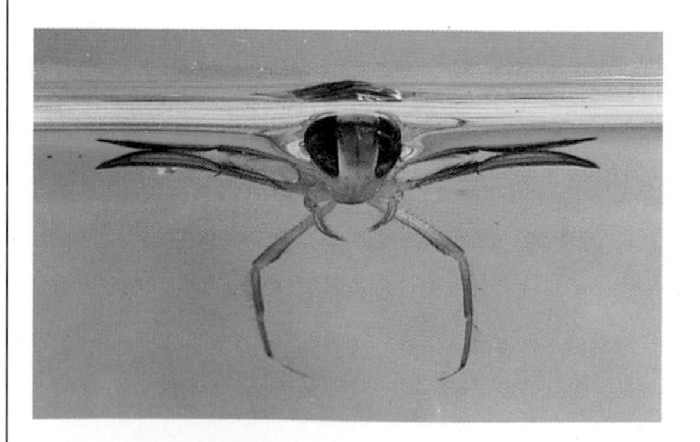

ROWING ALONG
The lesser water boatman has flattened back legs fringed with hairs. It uses these to push itself along. This species swims right side up, but some water boatmen swim upside down.

WALKING ON WATER
Water has a thin "skin" that is held together by a force called surface tension. Pond-skaters are light enough to walk on the skin without falling through.

HEAD TO TAIL
Processionary moth caterpillars travel in long lines when they leave their nests to feed. If they are touched, their long hairs can cause a painful rash.

Power-packed legs
Muscles in the upper part of the legs provide most of the power for the jump.

Springy knees
A springlike mechanism in the knees increases the force of the jump.

MIGHTY KICK
Grasshoppers jump to avoid predators and to launch themselves into flight. Their powerful back legs flick backwards to push them into the air.

The Right Legs for the Job

A close look at an insect's legs often helps to show where it lives and how it gets around. Insects that live on the ground often have claws to grip rough surfaces, or flat pads if they live on sand. Beetles that live on smooth leaves have broad feet with brushlike hairs, but those that live on hairy leaves have tiny claws to help them grip individual hairs. Many water insects have hairs along their legs. On a pond-skater, these hairs repel water and prevent the insect from sinking.

Water insect

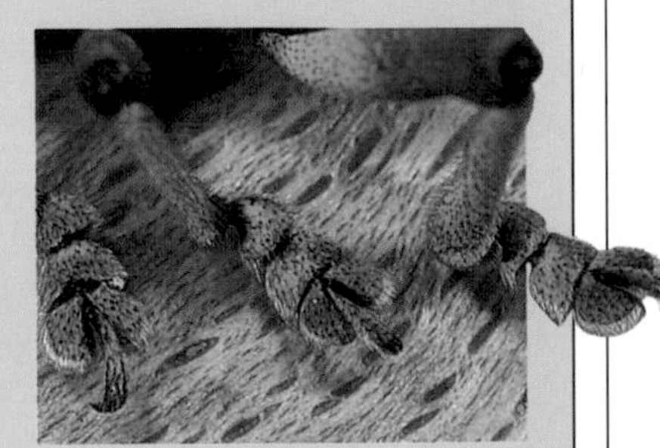

Ground insect

Discover more in True Bugs

Making Contact

In every insect's life, there are times when it has to make contact with other members of its species. It may need to warn of danger, to attract a mate, or to prove that it is not an enemy but a friend. Many insects communicate by sight, and they often use bright colors or patterns to identify themselves. After dark, most insects are hard to see, but fireflies are easy to spot. They make their own light, and flash coded signals to one another through the dark. For crickets, cicadas and some smaller insects, sound provides a way to contact a mate. Unlike sight, sound works during the day and night, and allows an insect to stay hidden while it broadcasts its call. Insects often use touch and taste to communicate when they meet, but they can also make contact by smell. Some of their scents waft a long way through the air, while others mark the ground to show where they have been.

Male firefly

LIGHTS IN THE NIGHT
Fireflies are small beetles that make contact using a pale-greenish light. The males flash as they fly overhead and the females—which are often wingless—flash back from the ground.

Female firefly

The Honeybee Dance

When a worker honeybee finds a good food source, it returns to the hive to pass on the news. It tells the other honeybees the distance and location of the food through a special figure eight dance. If the food is far away from the hive, the honeybee does a waggle in the middle of the figure eight (as shown below). The speed of the waggle tells the honeybees how far they must fly to find the food. The angle of the waggle shows the honeybees where the food is in relation to the sun.

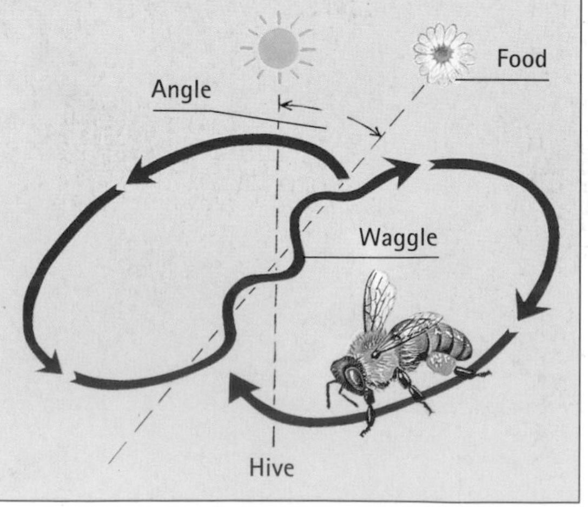

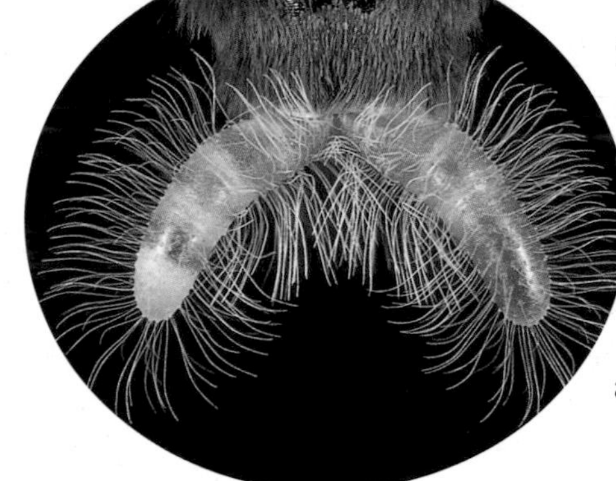

SCENTED MOTH
The male tiger moth attracts females by a scent called a pheromone, which is released into the air by two glands in the abdomen. These fold away when not in use.

SOUND SIGNALS
A grasshopper calls by scraping its back legs against the hard edges of its front wings. This causes the wings to vibrate and make a sound. This process is called stridulation.

TOUCH AND TASTE
When two ants meet, they touch each other briefly with their antennae. This tells them if they are from the same nest, and passes on the taste of any food they have found.